GW00381824

A BOOT UP

DERWENTWATER

Keith Wood

First published in Great Britain in 2009

Front cover: *Derwentwater* © Keith Wood

British Library Cataloguing-in-Publication Data
A CIP record for this title is available from the British Library

ISBN 978 1 906887 13 1

PiXZ Books
Halsgrove House, Ryelands Industrial Estate,
Bagley Road, Wellington, Somerset TA21 9PZ
Tel: 01823 653777
Fax: 01823 216796
email: sales@halsgrove.com

An imprint of Halstar Ltd, part of the Halsgrove group of companies
Information on all Halsgrove titles is available at: www.halsgrove.com

Printed and bound by Grafiche Flaminia, Italy

Contents

How to use this book

The third largest of the Cumbrian lakes, Derwentwater is surrounded by some of the Lake District's most beautiful scenery. Known as the 'Queen of the Lakes' nestling between the mountains in the Borrowdale Valley and next to the town of Keswick, it offers easily accessible walking for all abilities.

Due to the vast amounts of silt washed down from the surrounding fells over the centuries, Derwentwater is a shallow lake and the first to freeze during cold spells in the winter. The surrounding woodlands are spectacular throughout the year and several are designated Sites of Special Scientific Interest, including Castle Head Wood, the Ings,

and Great Wood visited in this book. Much of the area was acquired by the National Trust in its early days and a memorial stone to one of its founders, Canon Rawnsley, can be found on the footpath from the Keswick Landings to Friar's Crag. Much of the work of the National Trust involves conserving the precious habitats existing around the lake and in the Borrowdale Valley, whilst supporting farming and maintaining the area's characteristic stone walls and buildings.

Accessible from the M6 Motorway at Junction 40, and the A66 to Keswick, information about public transport from Penrith Station is provided by Traveline -

the services are frequent. The start points for several of the walks are from Keswick (Walks 1, 2, 3), others will need private cars.

Offering visitors many opportunities to access different points around the lake, the Keswick Launch Company provides trips around the lake calling at seven lakeshore jetties. (Walk 2 makes use of the 'Walkers' Special' to Hawes End, below Catbells). The launches operate throughout the seasons. Further details including timetables and special events are available from The Keswick Launch Company, 29 Manor Park, Keswick 017687 72263;
www.keswick-launch.co.uk.

The majority of walks in this book are relatively easy to moderate and offer delightful walking in this beautiful and varied landscape. For the more adventurous Walks 8 and 10 give a taste of true, mountain walking.

Each route is graded from Easy to More Challenging with further details of distance, height ascended and the type of terrain covered, to help with decisions of which walk to choose. The majority of the walks have details of refreshments and facilities available — usually at the end. However for some this requires a minor detour or short car journey.

All ten walks are covered by the Ordnance Survey Explorer Map OL4: The English Lakes, North-Western area, and Harvey's Lakeland Central and Lakeland West Maps. The maps in this book are only an outline version of each walk and the detail provided by the OS maps puts each route in context.

Every year tens of thousands of visitors enjoy the fells with the vast majority coming to no harm. However there are many cases each year where walkers are injured, get lost or find themselves in some other kind difficulty requiring the assistance of the Mountain Rescue Services. A few simple precautions should help avoid any problems:

- If you are unsure about your fitness start with the walks graded Easy and work your way up to More Challenging.
- Wear suitable footwear - properly fitted walking boots are recommended for all the walks.
- Take suitable clothing; the weather in the Lake District can change very quickly, take a waterproof and extra warm layers to wear.
- Take plenty to eat and drink en route, dehydration and lack of nourishment can lead to fatigue and mistakes being made.
- An outline map illustrates each walk but a full map is an essential part of walking equipment.
- Inform someone of your planned route and expected return time.
- Check the weather forecast in advance and only take to the more challenging routes on clear days.
- And finally keep to the paths and watch where you are putting your feet — most accidents are caused by careless slips!

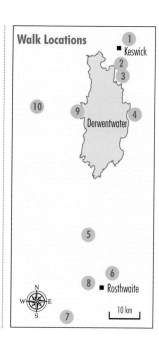

Walk Locations

Keswick

Derwentwater

Rosthwaite

N W E S

10 km

Key to Symbols Used

Level of difficulty:

Easy 🌿

Fair 🌿 🌿

More challenging 🌿 🌿 🌿

Map symbols:

 Park & start

Tarred Road

- - - - - Footpath

■ Building

6

1 Latrigg

Enjoy a full length view of the lake and Borrowdale from this popular viewpoint

Level: 🥾 🥾
Length: 5 ½ miles (9km)
Ascent: 1000 feet (300m)
Terrain: Easy start along the disused railway trackbed, followed by fair pull up to the top of Latrigg and a gradual descent.
Park & start: Car Park at rear of old Railway Station.
Start ref: GR 267 239.
Refreshments & facilities: Toilets at the Car Park. Keswick Country House Hotel adjacent to the Car Park.

This route makes use of the footpath created when the Lake District National Park Authority acquired part of the former Cockermouth to Penrith Railway after it closed in 1972. During improvements to the busy A66 much of the track was destroyed but this section between Keswick and Threlkeld, passing through the lovely Greta Gorge, has remained untouched. Passing through peaceful woodland, attractive throughout the year, with interesting man-made features, it seems a world away from the busy main road to the

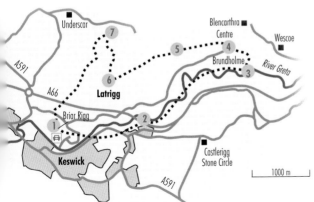

Northern and Western Lakes and the bustling tourist mecca of Keswick. Along the route are several information plaques giving information on both the heritage and natural history of the area. From this low level path, the track ascends Latrigg giving spectacular views of the area covered by the walks in this book and therefore makes an excellent starting point. Beyond Keswick the full length of Derwentwater stretches south with Walla Crag above the lake on the left, Catbells on the right and the beautiful Borrowdale Valley beyond framed by the cliff-face of Great End on the horizon.

1 Park in the free car park next to **Keswick Spa**, behind the old railway station. Take the bridlepath along the former railway trackbed, heading east away from the Spa. The route which is also part of the Coast to Coast cycle route goes through the outskirts of Keswick and heads towards the A66. Just before passing under the A66 there is a cast iron sculpture celebrating the Coast to Coast route, erected as part of the Millennium Project. Follow the path as it goes under the road (A66).

2 On entering the woods the first section is a high level boardwalk above the River Greta. Pass the platform of the former bobbin mill at **Low Brierly**. The track follows the line of the River Greta along the valley, criss-crossing the river with a series of bridges as the waters meander beneath.

Boardwalk above the Greta

C2C Cycle Way signpost

3 Opposite a small stone railway hut before another bridge crosses the river, there is to the left an iron gate with a small wooden walkers' gate next to it. Go through crossing a small field. Blencathra is straight ahead. Through a second set of gates onto the small narrow road, turn left and immediately the road starts to wind its way up the hillside. From the road the route up to **Latrigg** can be seen quite clearly to the left and beyond in the distance Causey Pike, Sail, Eel Crag. Keep following the farm track up the hill. Through an iron gate, the road then forks - keep to the left hand track, the other heads down into the valley. Keep straight towards Latrigg. Along the path there is a full view straight down the Newlands Valley to Robinson with High Stile and Red Pike on the horizon.

4 At another fork again keep to the left. Almost immediately the track forks again; to the left down through **Brundholme Woods**, but take the route over a stile next to a five bar gate with the signpost 'Skiddaw 4 miles'. Follow this track as it then climbs towards **Latrigg**. The tourist path up to Skiddaw can be seen on the right. This is now a steady climb to the top of **Latrigg**.

Skiddaw from Latrigg

Newlands Valley across Derwentwater

⑤ At a gate through a fence, where the track follows along the side of a wooded area head to the left up the grassy bank following a wide fairly indistinct track. After a few yards over the grass the path becomes visible swinging out up the ridge to the right. Eventually pass through a wooden gate follow the track onto the top of **Latrigg**.

⑥ The well worn path hugs the top of **Latrigg** until, at the front edge, there is a seat and the most spectacular views over the town of Keswick itself and Derwentwater beyond. To the right Bassenthwaite Lake lies in between a patchwork of fields and hedges. The extensive views follow all the way round from the Hellvellyn ridge on the left, the full length of Derwentwater with Catbells, Robinson, Hindscarth, Causey Pike and Grisedale to the right and round to Skiddaw behind. The path swings round to the right heading towards Skiddaw. As the main limited mobility path continues straight ahead towards Skiddaw, take the Public Footpath route to the left. At a further fork in the footpath keep to the right which is the wider more worn path.

⑦ At an isolated stone gatepost the path swings around back on itself now heading down towards **Keswick**. At a T junction take the path down to the left as it swings around and heads towards Keswick. At a junction beneath some trees with a couple of stone gateposts, one upright and the other laid down, take the lower track to the right. Through a gate exiting Latrigg Woods, head onto Spooney Green Lane and the bridge over the busy A66. On reaching the end of Spooney Green Lane, turn left and head back to **Keswick Spa**.

The mill at Low Briery provided wooden bobbins in vast quantities for the textile industry of Lancashire and Yorkshire. The stems of young trees were cut down near to ground level and then new shoots would emerge to be harvested again after about 20 years. Evidence of 'coppicing' can still be seen in the surrounding woods.

Keswick and Derwentwater from Latrigg

2 **Derwentwater Shoreline**

Cruise across the lake followed by a return by the shoreline path

Level: 🥾
Length: 5¾ miles (9km)
Ascent: Negligible
Terrain: Clear lakeside paths.
Park & start: Theatre by the Lake Car Park in Keswick.
Start ref: GR 265 229.
Refreshments & facilities: Wide choice available in Keswick.
Lodore Hotel (half-way round)
www.keswick-launch.co.uk

The full circuit around Derwentwater involves some unavoidable road walking and a walk through the town of Keswick. This shorter route takes in the best two thirds of the circuit avoiding the road walking. This shortening is made possible by taking a trip on one of the lake's launches from the Keswick Landings across to the Hawse End landing stage. The route then follows the shoreline crossing the delta at the foot of the lake on the newly refurbished boardwalk made from recycled plastic bottles! The walk finishes by visiting the famous Friar's Crag viewpoint which gives a full length view down the lake towards the Jaws of Borrowdale.

13

① Park at the Theatre by the Lake Car Park in Keswick, and walk down to the **Keswick Landings** past the Theatre. Start by taking the cruise across the end of the lake, passing by Derwent Island and disembarking at **Hawse End** at the foot of Catbells.

Crossing to Hawse End

Hawse End Landings

② Leave the jetty and immediately pick up the lakeside path on the left just above the shoreline. The path leaves the shoreline for a while and joins a wide surfaced path with Catbells above. Pass through a gate now back at the shoreline to enter mixed oak and pine woods - **Brandlehow Woods**. Pass by "the hand in the woods", a carving of a hand celebrating 100 years of the National Trust in Brandlehow Woods in 2002- entitled Entrust. Beautiful easy walking along the lakeshore through the woods beneath the oak trees.

3 Pass by **High Brandlehow Landing Stage**. The path splits at this point: take the left fork which continues to hug the shoreline around the spoil heaps. Pass Brandlehow Cottage and through a gate, soon arriving at a junction. Take the right fork and continue on the wide track.

4 Arriving at the Warren, a slate built cottage, on the right hand side of the track, turn left along a footpath through the wood indicated by a yellow arrow waymarker. This is part of the Cumbria Way. Once through a gate, the terrain opens out silver birches and myrtle and bracken as the end of the lake is reached.

Derwentwater Landings

Follow the well used boardwalk section over the marshy ground. From the boardwalk there is a great view down the full length of Derwentwater to **Skiddaw**. Cross the footbridge over the River Derwent and continue on the track heading towards the Borrowdale road. This section may be impassable after heavy rain.

5 Through the gate onto the Borrowdale road, turn left

Hand in Brandlehow Woods

and walk on the path beside the road. Just before reaching the **Lodore Hotel**, cross the road and follow the permitted path around the back of the hotel, signed to Keswick and Lodore Falls. Follow the path around the back of the hotel, cross over the beck using the iron footbridge. Upon entering the woods the path splits for a minor detour to visit the famous **Lodore Falls**, returning to the main path through the trees just above the road.

6 The path emerges opposite the National Trust's Kettlewell Car Park. Cross the road and pick up the lakeshore path on the left hand side of the road, initially just above the water's edge. Continue walking along the eastern shore crossing the wooden footbridge over **Ashness Gill**.

Lodore Falls

7 At **Ashness Bridge Landing Stage**, either keep to the shoreline or go onto the roadside footpath for this next section - access along the shoreline can be difficult when the water level is high. Directly beneath **Falcon Crag**, a number of paths can be taken to rejoin the shoreline path. Follow the shoreline path again, through the woods.

Boardwalk

Bridge over River Derwent

8 Follow the wide stony beach at **Calf Close Bay** heading towards the split rock sculpture. Passing the Centenary Stone, a split rock sculpture to commemorate 100 years of the National Trust, continue walking to the trees on the headland. Through the trees, go through a gate onto a well laid path with green pastures to the right. Approaching Lords Island close to the shore, the path swings away from the lake to go around Stable Hills cottages and over a cattle grid.

9 Follow the lane and after a short distance take the walkers' gate down on the left, heading into

The Ings on a good dry path through this marshy woodland area. Leave The Ings and continue through pasture land heading towards **Friar's Crag**, the famous viewpoint. Pass through a gate and take the narrow steps up to the left through the woods to enjoy the view from Friar's Crag, passing by the monument to John Ruskin.

Acorns

John Ruskin described Friar's Crag as being one of the three most beautiful scenes in Europe. It is believed to have got its name from being an embarkation point for monks making pilgrimages to St Herbert's Island, home of an anchorite (religious hermit) in the 7th century.

Finally take the busy path and road back to the **Keswick Landings** passing the Theatre by the Lake and to the Car Park.

Launch on Derwentwater

3 **Walla Crag**

Walk up the famous viewpoint of Walla Crag overlooking the lake

There are a total of six or seven high level viewpoints overlooking

Derwentwater in this collection of walks and this is one of the best. The walk also passes through no less than five areas of woodland showcasing the environmental diversity of the area. Starting immediately through Cockshot Wood, the route next passes through Castle Head Wood taking in the top of this ancient volcanic plug. After following the woods edging Brockle Beck the route follows the open fellside before descending into Great Wood. Finally the route passes through the marshy woodland known as The Ings on the edge of the lake.

Level: 🥾
Length: 5 miles (8km)
Ascent: 1200 feet (360m)
Terrain: Steady climb to Walla Crag with steep descent.
Park and start: Park at Theatre by the Lake Car Park in Keswick
Start ref: GR 265 229.
Refreshments & facilities: Theatre by the Lake; Keswick.

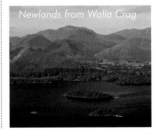

Newlands from Walla Crag

From the Car Park follow the road past the theatre towards Keswick Landings. After about 100 yards take the footpath off up to the left signed 'Public Footpath to Cockshot Wood'. This gravel path shortly splits three ways; take the middle path through the trees. Emerging at the edge of the wood, go through a gate and onto the narrow footpath between two fields, heading towards the road.

Cross straight over the busy Borrowdale Road and enter the wood through a narrow stone stile. After heading left for 10 yards, the path divides and starts to head up to the right into **Castle Head Woods**. Rising beneath the oak and beech trees, swing to the right at the

Keswick from Castle Head

margins of the wood and continue rising. At a wooden bench head off to the right again up through the trees to gain access to a stunning viewpoint over the lake towards Catbells and a view of Keswick. A plaque on the top gives the directions and names of all the surrounding fells. Retrace the route to pick up the main path again running along the edge of the wood. The path descends down the other side and reaching the edge of the wood go through a kissing gate

onto a surfaced path between fields emerging onto a road.

Turn right to walk along the road as it gently rises with the houses on the left and open views to the right. The road ends at Springs Farm, cross the bridge over **Brockle Beck**. Passing some farm buildings to the left, approach a wooden five bar gate and walkers' gate and enter the woods beside Brockle Beck. Follow the wide stony track up through these once coppiced woods with the beck tumbling down on the left. At a T junction of tracks, turn right and continue heading uphill signed 'Rakefoot Farm, Walla Crag and Castlerigg Stone Circle'. Pass the communications mast and follow the steadily rising path straight on towards Castlerigg and

Derwentwater from Castle Head

Footbridge over Brockle Beck

Walla Crag. Be aware of the steep drop down to the beck on the left, especially if accompanied by small children or dogs. Via a kissing gate, continue through the trees to arrive at a narrow wooden footbridge to cross back over Brockle Beck. Follow the path up the field and through a gate to arrive at a surfaced lane.

4 Turn right and walk along the lane towards **Rakefoot**. Where the road forks take the right path signed to 'Walla Crag'. At the end of the road cross the beck over the wooden footbridge and continue on the Public Footpath signed to 'Walla Crag'. The path passes through a gate and continues with the drystone wall on the right for the last pull up to **Walla Crag**. At a large pile of stones there is a kissing gate through the wall. Take this route to walk along the front edge of Walla Crag and enjoy the best views as the path crosses the heather-clad slopes.

5 The top of **Walla Crag** marked by a small cairn of stones is soon reached. Enjoy the magnificent views from here looking down onto **Calf Close Bay** and the four main islands of Derwentwater. From here keep following the path back to the wall and pass through a stile in the wall turning right to head gently downhill. Keep the drystone wall close on the right hand side. Approaching the top of Cat Gill, take the well-made path for the steep descent down to the lakeshore. Reaching the bottom, turn right and continue on the path heading towards Great Wood Car Park, walking through the lower reaches of **Great Wood**. Keep to the path ignoring paths off to the left and right on the way to Great Wood Car Park.

6 Upon reaching the Car Park walk along the road to the entrance of the Car Park signed No Entry for Cars. The busy Borrowdale road is just 20 yards away. Cross the road and down the steps and onto a path which leads through the woods. Upon reaching the main path through the woods turn right over a wooden footbridge and continue on the clear path through the woods adjacent to the road, signed 'Keswick 1 mile'. The

The Theatre by the Lake has its origins in the "Blue Box Theatre" - the touring venue of Century Theatre - which occupied the site from 1976 until its removal to make way for the permanent Theatre by the Lake in 1996. In a unique, dramatic location, the theatre has produced over 5000 performances to date.

Calf Close Bay from Walla Crag

path arrives at a lane by the road with a sign 'Public Footpath' pointing down to the left heading towards the lake. This wide lane progresses along the margins of **The Ings**.

7 At a slight bend in the lane take the gate on the right hand side into **The Ings**. Follow this path as it now follows the shoreline path, passing Friar's Crag and returning to the Keswick Landings and the Theatre by the Lake.

Edge of Walla Crag

Reflections from Friar's Crag

4 Great Wood to Ashness Bridge

An easy walk to an iconic viewpoint, returning above Falcon Cragg

The view from Ashness Bridge must have featured on more cake and biscuit tins, calendars, magazine and book covers than any other in the Lake District and so I couldn't find it in my heart to write a book of leisure walks around Derwentwater without including a visit to the iconic viewpoint. But this walk has so much more than just Ashness Bridge. Starting from Great Wood the route takes a leisurely stroll along the eastern flanks of the lake with great views across the lake, before arriving at Ashness Bridge. The return climbs

Level:

Length: 3 miles (4.8km)

Ascent: 900 feet (270m)

Terrain: Easy walking to Ashness Bridge followed by a stiff climb and steep descent.

Park and start: National Trust Great Wood Car Park.

Start ref: GR 271 214.

Refreshments & facilities: Keswick.

to a magnificent viewpoint above Falcon Crag looking down onto the lake finally dropping back down to Great Wood down the narrow ravine of Cat Gill.

① Park in the National Trust Great Wood Car Park on the shores of **Derwentwater**. From the ticket machine walk about 20 yards along the road towards the exit to reach a path forking off to the left from the road with a finger post marked 'Footpath', walking on a clear path with a gentle incline through the woods with the tall pine trees towering into the sky. Ignoring a path to the right and another to the left, keep straight on. After a while the tumbling waters of **Cat Gill** are heard.

② Whilst the main path swings up to the left, keep heading straight on across a wooden footbridge over Cat Gill. Continue on the footpath on the opposite bank initially heading downhill next to a drystone wall on the right before the path swings around to the left away from the wall and continues heading south. The great buttress of **Falcon Crag** comes into view up on the left and the view opens out across Derwentwater to Catbells, Maiden Moor and High Spy on the opposite bank of the lake. Directly

Bridge over Cat Gill

beneath Falcon Crag pass by a number of large boulders which have fallen from the rockface in centuries gone by. Continuing along this very pleasant path on the level, a green plateau is reached with a large stone cairn and signpost marking a fork in the path down to road to the right; keep going on the left fork signed for 'Ashness Bridge'. The path gently rises as it continues heading towards **Ashness Bridge**. Shortly the packhorse bridge and falls behind come into view in the distance.

③ Reaching a drystone wall with a gate through it, the return route that is to be followed doubles back on itself up to the left up through the bracken up the fellside. But it would be silly not to visit Ashness

Ashness Bridge

Bridge. So for a minor detour go through the gate through the wall and keep to the path for the last 50 yards to reach the bridge and falls to enjoy the iconic view towards **Skiddaw**.

4 Having taken the obligatory pictures of Ashness Bridge, retrace the steps back up to the drystone wall, head through the gate and now take the narrow path to the right between the bracken heading up the fellside. The path slants up the fellside gradually ascending to the ridge. Ever expansive views are achieved as height is gained along Derwentwater with the stretch of water beyond - Bassenthwaite Lake. Heading up the fellside a wire fence is crossed using a wooden stile and

Ashness Bridge is one of the Lake District's most iconic and photographed scenes. Throughout the seasons the ever-changing landscape provides the perfect back-drop for this fine packhorse bridge, crossing the Ashness Gill as it tumbles down from remote Watendlath to Derwentwater below.

continue following the muddy path up the fellside. Where the path meets another from right to left, turn left and continue on the now stony path gently rising. Walking along the edge of the upland plateau, the path continues to rise steadily approaching the highest point on the walk. Take a 15 yard detour to a lofty station overlooking the lake for the best views over the lake below. Return to the main path which swings around to the right and then back left to safely make its way around the top of the **Cat Gill** ravine.

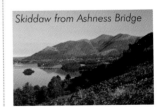

Skiddaw from Ashness Bridge

5 Having rounded the top of the ravine and then crossed a stream which is the top of Cat Gill, the path forks. Take the minor but clear path to the left heading down towards a drystone wall with the upper part of Cat Gill on the left. The descent starts with the rushing waters of Cat Gill on the left, the boundary wall of **Great Wood** in front and the last clear views across the lake. The narrow trod joins the main path just before the wall, head left downhill with the wall now on the right. Ignore a stile through

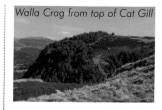

Walla Crag from top of Cat Gill

the wall and keep heading down the main path. The descent steepens on a well built and stepped path. Keep to the steep but safe path as it descends the ravine. Pass through a kissing gate in a wire fence to enter the woods. Through another kissing gate the path continues descending through the woods with the gill on the left. Shortly the bridge across the gill used at the start of the walk is reached; all that remains is to retrace the route back to the right through the lower parts of Great Wood to the start point.

Across Derwentwater from above Falcon Cragg

5 King's How & the Bowder Stone

Walk to a commanding viewpoint, returning past a geological wonder

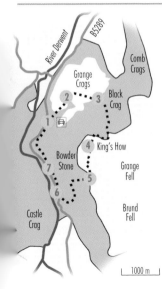

Level: 🥾 🥾
Length: 2 ½ miles (3.7km)
Ascent: 950 feet (290m)
Terrain: A steep climb to a fine viewpoint with an equally steep descent.
Park and start: National Trust Bowder Stone Car Park.
Start ref: GR 253 169.
Refreshments & facilities: Available in the village of Rosthwaite; Keswick.

A tourist attraction for over 200 years the origins of the Bowder Stone are the source of much debate. Possibly an 'erratic' – a stone carried by glaciers from a different area at the end of the last ice age, it is more likely to be the result of a massive rock-fall from the cliffs above. In the late 18th century local landowner Joseph Pocklington bought the site and started to encourage people to visit. He built Bowderstone Cottage to house a resident guide, the Druid Stone opposite the cottage, a small chapel which is now used as a climbing hut and erected the first ladders to give access to the top of the stone.

Heather on King's How

① From the National Trust Bowder Stone Car Park, leave through one of the pair of gates at the back of the upper Car Park. Take the left hand gate on a fairly clear path through the birch trees heading towards a displaced giant slab of rock,

Top of King's How

Autumn colours on Kings How

fallen from the crag on the right at some time in the past - almost like a mini Bowder Stone itself. Continue on the path through the light woodland, gently rising to the remains of an old slate quarry.

② Follow the clear path forward round the base of **King's How**, swinging around to the right

shortly after leaving the slate quarry. After a short climb, a small grassy plateau is reached, marked by another huge rock fallen from the crag. Continue on through the bracken slightly downhill now heading towards a drystone wall. Through a gate in the wall, continue to follow the path through the birch trees on these lower slopes.

3 The path crosses a stream before the real climbing begins. The path markedly steepens to start to head up the fellside through the trees. Repaired in many places, this popular lakeland path rises relentlessly through the mixed woodland on its journey to the heather-covered upper slopes. After the steep climb, the path levels out and crosses a wooded glade passing into the open and continues to swing around to the right. Ignore a stile over a fence to the left and keep on the stony path which starts to rise again. After another climb through the trees the path flattens out and opens out onto a heather-clad bowl with the rocky heather-faced summit to the front. This bowl is marshy in places but the path skirts around on the right, keeping the feet dry. Cross over the stream flowing out of the marsh and the path once again starts to climb. The route levels out on a grassy path through more silver birch and starts to swing to the left just before a wall and then climbs again. Continue on the path to the summit passing by a stone plaque to King Edward VII.

4 The rocky summit is marked by a small stone cairn and the views open out to the south, with the great mass of **Glaramara** in the mid ground, to the South with Castle Crag nestling in the valley below and to the north Derwentwater and Skiddaw. From the summit the path continues over the fell heading

Derwentwater from King's How

south towards Glaramara, immediately starting to lose height and in the middle ground you can see a drystone wall which is the next point on the route. Dropping down the slope the path levels off as it meets a right to left path with a lonely silver birch. Take the right hand path heading towards **Borrowdale** through the bracken on a green path. The path swings back round to the left and continues heading south towards the wall, losing height all the time.

5 The path soon reaches the drystone wall, turn right and continue on the path heading down the fellside with the wall on your left. Before long re-enter the upper reaches of the Borrowdale woodland, the path descending steeply down the fellside

Looking north from King's How

into Borrowdale. Pass through a collapsed drystone wall and continue heading down the steep sided slopes. The path heads south again towards Glaramara which feels like the wrong direction, but stick with it as the path reassuringly swings back around to the right. The busy road at the bottom can soon be seen.

Descending from King's How

"In loving memory of King Edward VII, Grange Fell is dedicated by his sister Louise as a sanctuary of rest and peace here may all beings gather strength and in scenes of beautiful nature a case for gratitude and love to God giving them courage and vigour to carry on his will."

6 The path reaches the road at a stile over a wire fence with the river at the other side of the road. Cross the stile and turn right to walk beside the road around the corner. At a footpath sign 'Public Bridleway Bowder Stone', pass through a gate on the right side of the road to pick up

Sign to the Bowder Stone

the clear stony path running parallel to the road through the trees towards the **Bowder Stone** and the start point.

7 At the Bowder Stone, climb the steps to the top before continuing on the path to return to the Car Park on a well laid disabled access track through the trees.

The Bowder Stone

6 Watendlath & Dock Tarn

Visit two high level tarns and a crag offering views of upper Borrowdale

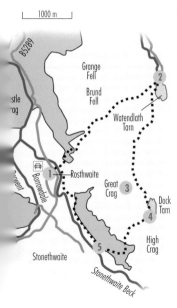

This walk follows a route taking in a famous tarn with its ancient settlement, another high level tarn and a crag giving views of upper Borrowdale and the towering heights of Great Gable and the Scafells. The return journey follows a steep path down through attractive deciduous woodland to the valley floor, before hugging close to the river back to the start.

From the Old Norse 'vatn-endi-hlaoa', meaning water-end barn, the secluded hamlet of Watendlath and its tarn is **one of the most scenic and often photographed Lake District locations.**

Level: 🥾 🥾
Length: 5 ¼ miles (8.5km)
Ascent: 1630 feet (500m)
Terrain: A steady walk with some stiff gradients and a steep descent on a well-pitched path.
Park and start: National Trust Car Park in Rosthwaite.
Start ref: GR 257 148
Refreshments & facilities: Toilets, village shop, 'The Flock In' Yew Tree Farm, The Scafell Hotel, Rosthwaite; Caffle House Tearoom, Watendlath.

The tranquil tarn is a haven for anglers. Water from Watendlath Tarn flows into the beck and eventually feeds Lodore Falls, and ends up in Derwentwater. The smaller Dock Tarn is located high

Borrowdale on the ascent

above the **Borrowdale Valley** in an idyllic setting near the summit of the 'Wainwright' fell of **Great Crag** between **Watendlath**, **Stonethwaite** and **Rosthwaite**.

(1) In the small village of **Rosthwaite**, park in either the National Trust Car Park, or the adjacent Borrowdale Institute. Turn left at the car park entrance heading back towards the main road and the village store. Walk 20 yards along the road past the bus shelter, almost immediately taking the lane off the right, signposted 'Public Bridleway Watendlath 1 ½ miles'. Follow the surfaced lane and once over the bridge take the path to the left again signed 'Public Bridleway Watendlath'. Pass behind the back of Dina Hogas

Camping Barn into a walled lane heading up towards **Watendlath**. Through a gate, the clear path now starts to gently climb, meandering up the fellside. Through another gate and take the clearly signed left hand fork and continue to rise up the fellside. The path flattens out and crosses through another gate in the stone wall as the watershed is reached and the ridge of the Central Fells comes into view. Great Crag with its little rocky pinnacle can now be seen across to the right before the path drops down to the tarn at Watendlath.

(2) As the path reaches the shores of the tarn take a minor detour into the hamlet over the pack horse bridge. Return over the bridge continuing on the route round

the right hand shore of the tarn on the path heading towards **Dock Tarn** and **Great Crag**. The path starts to swing to right and left following the line of the wall on the right hand side, heading gently up towards Great Crag. Crossing over the beck which flows into the tarn, follow a small arrowed sign pointing up to the right next to the beck, ignoring the route straight on. Through a kissing gate, immediately swing around to the left

Looking down onto Watendlath

Looking back to Dale Head and Rigghead Quarries across Borrowdale on the ascent

this time following an advisory sign to avoid erosion of the wetland area, and follow the little arrow to the left keeping to the main path. Pass a sheep fold on the left and the shapely summit of Great Crag comes into view

straight ahead. At a T junction head to the left following the arrow to Dock Tarn and **Stonethwaite**, keeping to the path as it rises through wetland. The rocky path meanders through the undulations below Great Crag, crossing

Watendlath Bridge

Watendlath Tarn

over another stream and through a kissing gate in the intake wall before facing a steep climb on a pitched path. After quite a stiff little pull, the rocky path levels off through the heather and continues on to Dock Tarn.

(3) For those who wish to make a minor excursion to the twin peaks of Great Crag, a path heads off right through the heather just before a vertical rock monolith. The indistinct path eventually leads to the southernmost pile of stones, a cairn marking the higher of the twin peaks of Great Crag and the view opens looking down onto Borrowdale to the south and to the north, Watendlath Tarn and Skiddaw, a windfarm on the edge of the Solway

and beyond into Scotland. Rejoin the main path heading towards the blue waters of Dock Tarn.

(4) The path skirts around the shoreline of Dock Tarn and at its southern end starts to swing away and around to the right. Just before a

stream the path heads down and round to the right with the beck bubbling away on the left. Climb over a stile back through the intake wall, with the ghyll descending rapidly down a ravine on the left. The path starts to descend through the mixed woodland with **Stonethwaite Beck** running far below in the valley bottom. Continue on the well-pitched but steep path down through the woods. Near the bottom cross over another stile and continue walking through the oak woodland, emerging from the trees into the Stonethwaite Valley. Cross over a stile through the wall and meet the main track at the bottom of the valley.

Dock Tarn

The wetland areas above Watendlath are home to bog myrtle. This highly aromatic herb has antibacterial properties and has been used for decades to repel the wee biting beasties – midges! Definitely worth preserving as anyone who has been nibbled will testify!

Honister Pass on the descent

⑤ Turn right at the main track and follow the stony lane along the valley bottom back to **Rosthwaite**. The path rejoins the outward journey by the bridge over the river in the village.

Stonethwaite Valley from slopes of High Doat

(2) The path passes between the two highest points of **High Doat**. Visit each to fully appreciate the views. Looking to the south there is Great End, Scafell Pike and Great Gable and then to the north, Blencathra, Skiddaw and in the foreground our next destination, **Castle Crag**. Having explored the crags on either side of the path, return to the green

path and follow west. Where the path meets a wire fence swing to the left, climb over a stile through the wall and follow the path down the hillside across the valley to the beck, aiming for the ladder stile over the wall at the other side.

Castle Crag from High Doat

(3) Join the old miners' route/bridleway from **Grange** to **Honister**, turning right and following the path over the footbridge, continuing with the intake wall on your right-hand side towards Castle Crag. Over another bridge and then a little further

Footbridge over Scalehouse Gill

along through a gate in the wall, continue on the path heading towards the Jaws of Borrowdale. Cross a third footbridge over **Tongue Gill** and continue on the path.

 As the track starts to descend down towards **Derwent-**

water having just passed a complex of sheepfolds on the right, veer slightly to the right and follow the narrow path which starts to head up Castle Crag. On reaching a stone wall backed by beech trees cross over a stile in the wire fence and then over a ladder stile on the stone wall. The path then

zig-zags steeply through the slate spoil heaps towards the summit.

5 The only way off Castle Crag is to retrace the route back down the spoil heap. This time continue down past the stile taking the track to the right. Cross over a wooden stile in the wire fence and then down a ladder stile. Follow the track down to rejoin the main bridleway and turn right to head down towards **Grange**. Cross the beck at the bottom and enter the woodland around the base of Castle Crag.

6 Just before the river, at a fingerpost take the sign 'Public Footpath to Rosthwaite'. The footpath now follows the river. After a short distance, the path swings away from the river and up by a stonewall before pass-

Borrowdale from Castle Crag

ing through the gap in the wall next to a wooden post. Continue on through the wood, the path rising very gently between the trees. At the next fingerpost the path to **Rosthwaite** goes down to the left. Leave the woods through a kissing gate and continue on the path as it heads towards Rosthwaite.

⑦ At the stone bridge over the river, carry straight on, on the right hand bank. Cross over two wooden footbridges and then follow the narrow path between the fenced field and the bank of the river. Pass directly in front of some farm buildings and upon reaching the surfaced road turn right towards the Youth Hostel. Follow the sign 'Public Footpath to Seatoller'. Passing in front of the Youth Hostel the path then regains

the riverbank. A little further on, a chain provides a hand hold to help to negotiate a stretch of steep, smooth rocks. Scramble over the rocks heading to the left to follow the path around an outcrop. The track now levels out and follows around the edge of the wood with the wall to the left. Eventually the edge of the wood is reached and the path swings slightly uphill to meet the wall. Pass through, turning left and follow the track back to the National Trust Car Park at Seatoller.

Spoil heaps on Castle Crag

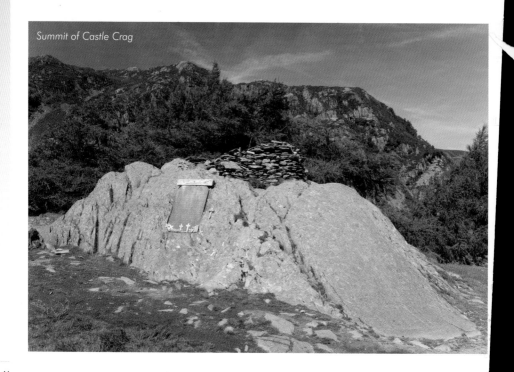

Summit of Castle Crag

8 High Spy & Borrowdale

A serious mountain expedition to the highest point in this collection of walks

Level: ♥ ♥ ♥

Length: 8 ½ miles (14km)

Ascent: 2400 feet (700m)

Terrain: A fairly tough fellwalk initially on riverside paths, surfaced lanes and finally high fell paths.

Park and start: National Trust Car Park in Rosthwaite.

Start ref: GR 258 149.

Refreshments & facilities: Toilets, village shop, 'The Flock In' Yew Tree Farm, The Scafell Hotel, Rosthwaite; Tearooms, Grange.

Whatever your motivation for going for a walk in the Lake District, be it to seek out the flora and fauna, the sense of achievement of climbing one of the high fells or to explore Lakeland's industrial heritage, this walk in Borrowdale has something for everyone. Starting in the busy little hamlet of Rosthwaite, the route initially follows the Cumbria Way along the banks of the River Derwent, before climbing up on to one of the best ridge routes in the north western fells, ascending to the summit of High Spy at over 2000 feet before

finally descending past the remains of Rigghead Quarries back down to the valley floor to return to Rosthwaite.

① Leave the Car Park and walk down the lane towards Yew Tree Farm. Follow the footpath sign to **Grange**, then the farm lane down to the River Derwent. Upon reaching the riverside the lane swings to the right, to arrive at a pack horse bridge over the river. Cross the bridge and turn right to continue on the track along the riverbank. Keep to the main path through a copse of oak trees and through a gate to enter the woods. At a Y junction take the right fork and twenty yards later turn right again following the Public Footpath sign to Grange. Continue through the woods, passing through a wall and back down towards the river. The path follows the course of the river to reach a lane past a campsite. At a T junction with a surfaced lane, turn right to walk into Grange.

River Derwent

② Emerge onto the road through Grange, turn left to follow the road around the south west corner of **Derwentwater**. Take care, this narrow stretch of road can be busy at certain times of year

③ Immediately past Manesty Holiday Cottages a path veers off to the left signed 'Public Footpath' which immediately starts to ascend the fellside on a clear path through the bracken. The path branches above **Manesty Woods**, where the real work of the day commences. Take the left path steeply rising heading up to **Hause Gate**. This well laid, recently repaired path up the side of **Maiden Moor** affords glorious views on a clear day across Derwentwater towards Keswick

Like many mines in the area, the Rigghead Quarries produced slate from levels cut deep into the fellside. Fascinating remains of this industrial heritage litter the area around the beck, however don't be tempted to enter the still open horizontal entrances – they are dangerous and should not be explored!

Newlands from Hause Gate

with Skiddaw and Blencathra in the distance give the excuse to be able to pause frequently for a breather!

(4) The path emerges at Hause Gate, turn left on the well worn path heading up to Maiden Moor. Upon reaching a cairn take the narrow, right hand trod which skirts the edge of the plateau. This gives the opportunity to look down into the

valley and across to **Hindscarth** and **Dalehead**. Passing the highest point of Maiden Moor, the path

Looking north from Maiden Moor

Summit of High Spy

commence the steep descent to **Borrowdale**, walking to the right of the gill through the abandoned slate

Top of Rigghead Quarries

rejoins the main path to head up to **High Spy**. Initially climbing again, the path finally levels off to reach the well built summit cairn of High Spy.

5 From High Spy simply keep on the main path, marked by cairns to start the descent down to the depression between High Spy and

Dalehead, with Dalehead Tarn clearly in view. Follow the stony path down, which is steep in places.

6 A faint track appears on the left in the direction of **Rosthwaite**, just above a minor tarn crossing marshy ground towards a fence and stile. Through the stile,

Tongue Gill and Rigghead Quarries

mine workings. Take the minor path off to the right to be able to further explore the industrial heritage at **Rigghead Hut** with the remains of some winding gear for transporting the slate down the valley. From the hut continue heading down. Upon meeting a wall go through the gate and continue down the initially stony track to arrive at the valley bottom and the river. Cross a stile beside one stream, and 10 yards later a second stream via a wooden footbridge, to follow the path beside the stream.

(7) Cross over a further footbridge with the Derwent now on the right. Only 15 yards further on turn right, back over the packhorse bridge crossed at the beginning of the walk to retrace the route back to **Rosthwaite**.

Borrowdale from Tongue Gill

9 Catbells

An ascent of the ever popular Catbells with great views either side of the ridge

No collection of walks around Derwentwater would be complete without a walk up the iconic Catbells. Start this walk either from Keswick taking the walkers' launch across the lake to Hawes End or park the car at the foot of the fell along the Portinscale to Grange road which runs along the western side of the lake. There is limited parking so an early arrival is necessary. At a hairpin bend at the foot of the ridge take a minor road off to Skelgill, where after a short distance a small parking area suitable for about 15 vehicles is found.

Level: 🐾 🐾
Length: 3 ¾ miles (6km)
Ascent: 1500 feet (450m)
Terrain: Steady climb up the ridge, steep descent and return along the level.
Park and start: Parking spaces at the fell-foot.
Start ref: GR 246 211.
Refreshments & facilities: Portinscale and Keswick.

Catbells from King's How

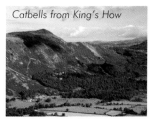

1 Take the clear footpath from the Car Park heading back towards the turn in the road running parallel with the road, with bracken on either side. Just above the road junction join another path coming up from the road on the left. Continue walking along the fellside on this well laid and hugely popular path which starts to rise gently along the flank of the fell to reach the end of the ridge. On reaching the nose of the ridge, the path swings around to the

Sheep on the slopes of Catbells

Beatrix Potter, the famous children's author and illustrator lived in the Lake District. On her death she bequeathed most of her property to the National Trust thus preserving much of the area for the nation. Mrs Tiggywinkle, her famous hedgehog character, lived near Little Town in the Newlands Valley below Catbells.

right and branches off at a T junction to climb fairly steeply to the right straight up the ridge with great views already opening out. This well built and repaired path zigzags up the front of the ridge gaining height. Keep to the main path and avoid taking any of the shortcuts. The path levels off for the first time before resuming the climb up a fairly eroded section leading to a plaque dedicated to "Thomas Arthur Leonard". Continue up the little rocky scramble just above the plaque using hands to support over rock made smooth and slippery with use, before the path levels off for a second time.

2 After another little climb the path levels off again for a longer stretch along the ridge with outstanding views down to the left of Derwentwater and to the right full length views along the **Newlands Valley** with Robinson prominent in the centre ground. The route continues with a longish flat stretch along the shoulder losing a little height. Drop

Stonycroft Gill from Catbells

down to a little col before resuming the upward journey for the last pull to the top. The route ahead can be seen clearly. After another little rise tackle the final, fairly steep climb up to the rocky summit. The path loses its clarity up the loose, shaley surface, but follow any one of the numerous routes continuing uphill all arriving at the same point.

(3) From the airy summit, with fine views on both sides, the route continues in a straight forward manner. Follow the only path along the line of the ridge which immediately starts losing height heading towards **Maiden Moor**. There is a good view now to the front left all along Borrowdale with King's How and Great Crag behind, and the green fields in

the valley bottom. This is easy walking, gently descending on this wide stony path, a chance to stretch the legs heading down to the col or depression between Catbells and Maiden Moor.

(4) As the depression is reached with its crossroads of paths, take the path to the left heading down towards Derwentwater. The path heads steeply down the flank of the fell on another repaired path, a bit like descending a staircase, with

Climbing the ridge

Looking back down the ridge

views down onto Derwentwater and across to Walla Crag. The path zig zags down and along the fellside walking towards the Jaws of Borrowdale, losing height all the way. Ignore the first muddy path heading off to the left, keeping on the main path. Pass a green platform which makes a good viewing station across the lake.

(5) On reaching a Y junction, the path splits into two, to the right continuing along to Grange and Borrowdale, but take the left fork on a

Hugh Walpole memorial

clear path now doubling back north heading towards Skiddaw, still losing some more height above a little plantation of pine trees on the right. At a T junction of paths by the wall, turn left again continuing on the clear path along the foot of Catbells. This is very pleasant walking along the level on the lower slopes of Catbells, with the lake below to the right. Pass a slate plaque and seat in memory of Sir Hugh Walpole of Brackenburn, giving a fine view across the lake to **Blencathra**.

Newlands from Catbells

Continue the easy walking along the fellside with the road below, looking across to Walla Crag and Bleaberry Fell.

(6) Just before some woodland, the path joins the road for 10 yards in front of an abandoned quarry. Beyond the quarry rejoin the path rising gently above the road. The path continues to climb gently for quite a long stretch to regain a couple of hundred feet, before levelling off to complete the journey along the level around the front of Catbells. Gradually lose the height again to meet up with the road at the end of the fell. Turn left along the road, swinging around the front to reach the hairpin bend heading around to **Portinscale**. Take the left turn and follow the road to **Skelgill** back to the Car Park.

Maiden Moor and Borrowdale from Catbells

10 Barrow & Outerside

A walk into the heart of the North Western Fells over two of the lower tops

Dominating the scene over the eastern Newlands Valley, these two mountains in miniature make for an ideal half day or family walk. Situated on the southern leg of the Coledale Horseshoe, they form a mini ridge themselves, with the summit of Outerside in particular being an excellent viewing platform to gain an

Level: 🥾 🥾 🥾
Length: 5 ½ miles (9km)
Ascent: 2100 feet (650m)
Terrain: Mine road to start, sometimes wet mid-section, returning on clear path down the ridge.
Park and start: Uzzicar, Newlands Valley. Park on the wide area off the road.
Start ref: GR 232 216.
Refreshments & facilities: The Swinside Inn, Newlands Valley.

appreciation of the surrounding fells. Once on the ridge there are spectacular views down into Coledale to the north and Newlands Valley to the south.

Grisedale Pike

Coledale Beck

Braithwaite

High Coledale

Barrow Gill

6

4 Barrow Door

5 Barrow

1 Uzzicar

Outerside 3

Stonycroft Gill

Stoneycroft

2

Causey Pike

Skelgill

1000 m

(1) Heading along the **Newlands Valley** from Braithwaite on the left above Uzzicar there is a large area off the roadside with plenty of space for parking which makes the ideal point to start this walk. Cross the road and immediately pick up the old mine track which heads up **Stonycroft Gill** to a long

Walking up Stonycroft Gill

Falls along Stonycroft Gill

abandoned Cobalt Mine. Initially the track proceeds parallel to the road beneath the slopes of Barrow towards **Causey Pike** with the Newlands Valley stretching away to the front. The well-built track starts to rise as it swings around to the right to go up the narrow gill between Barrow and Causey Pike. Follow the mine track gaining height all the while up the rowan-lined gill. At the top of the gill the path levels out and swings around to the left beneath **Outerside** past a large derelict sheepfold.

(2) Continue along the mine road walking in the direction of **Eel Crags** beyond the summit of Outerside until a small cairn is reached marking the beginning of a faint path leading back through the heather up to Outerside. This "back door" route avoids a direct frontal assault and a stiff climb through the heather. Doubling back, the path climbs up to the summit of Outerside,

Top of Stonycroft Gill

at **1863 feet (568m)** the highest point of the walk. From the summit an extensive panorama opens out to the north and east, looking across to Bassenthwaite, Skiddaw, Keswick and Blencathra, with the Pennines in the distance along the route of the A66. To the northwest the magnificent face of **Grisedale Pike** dominates the scene. From here most of the return route can be seen; along the ridge to the intermediate summit of Stile End, and from there down to Barrow Door, the col below Barrow, and the clear path over Barrow.

(3) First descend from Outerside to the depression, on a path which is steep in places with a loose surface, to reach the level which is marshy in places. Pick up one of the

paths up to **Stile End** through the heather, passing a small tarn. Climb up the gentle slope to the minor summit of Stile End, with a view down to the village of Braithwaite. Looking south there is a fine view of the distinctive outline of Causey Pike and the ridge to **Scar Crags**.

The rich geology of the mountains of the Lake District spawned a hive of industrial activity in previous centuries. Many of the valleys and fellsides are still riddled with the remains of these mine workings. Barrow had an extensive and very old lead mine, which also gave up small deposits of silver.

Sail and Eel Crag from Outerside

Grisedale Pike

(4) From Stile End summit, retrace the route for a couple of yards to find a narrow path down the front of the fellside to the col at **Barrow Door**. From the col take the clear path up to **Barrow**, the final summit of this gentle half day outing.

(5) From the summit of Barrow, with its outstanding views across **Derwentwater** and Keswick towards Skiddaw, the route follows the path straight down the ridge. Looking down to the right from the summit the start point in the valley below can be seen. Follow the wide heather lined path down the line of the ridge straight towards **Braithwaite**. As height is lost the heather diminishes to be replaced by bracken, now walking on smooth short cropped turf.

(6) At the bottom of the ridge there is a sign post at a junction of paths, take the right hand turn signed **Newlands**, along another wide grass path just above a pine wood around the foot of Barrow heading towards the start. The path follows the edge of the trees and descends to the road just before a large scree fall. All that is left is to walk back along the quiet road to the start.

Skiddaw from Outerside

Causey Pike and Stonycroft Gill from Barrow